D0116950

peace is every breath

also by thich nhat hanh

No Death, No Fear

Living Buddha, Living Christ

Fragrant Palm Leaves

Being Peace

For a Future to Be Possible

The Heart of the Buddha's Teaching

The Heart of Understanding

The Long Road Turns to Joy

Love in Action

The Miracle of Mindfulness

Old Path White Clouds

Peace Is Every Step

Anger

True Love

The Art of Power

Savor

a practice for our busy lives

peace is
every
breath

THICH NHAT HANH

calligraphy by thich nhat hanh

HarperOne
An Imprint of HarperCollinsPublishers

HarperOne

HarperCollins books may be purchased for educational, business, or sales promotional use. For information please write: Special Markets Department, HarperCollins Publishers, 10 East 53rd Street, New York, NY 10022.

HarperCollins website: http://www.harpercollins.com

HarperCollins®, 📖®, and HarperOne™ are trademarks of HarperCollins Publishers

FIRST EDITION

Library of Congress Cataloging-in-Publication Data is available.

ISBN 978–0–06–200581–6

11 12 13 14 15   RRD(H)   10 9 8 7 6 5 4 3 2 1

Waking up this morning, I smile.

Twenty-four brand-new hours are before me.

I vow to live fully each moment

and to look at all beings with eyes of compassion.

contents

author's note

When I was a young monk studying at the Buddhist institute, I always asked how the Buddha's teachings we studied could be applied in real life. I was convinced that the right practice of the teachings would help me, other people around me, and my country. The desire to learn "applied Buddhism" was very real and strong, but that expression was not used back then. The kind of Buddhist teachings and methods we learned at that time were difficult for young people like myself to put into practice, partly because of the language used to teach them and partly because they didn't directly address the sorts of suffering and difficulties that people in modern society were experiencing.

We needed concrete practices that could address the issues of poverty, social injustice, inequality, and national independence. In the Middle Ages, Buddhist teachings served my country and people very successfully, but if they were not renewed for the modern era, they would not be able to continue helping our society to be inspired and improved. So the challenge for us practitioners was to renew Buddhism.

When I became a young Dharma teacher, I tried to present Buddhism in a language that could be easily understood by people of my generation, and to present practices that could help them suffer less and have enough joy and peace to be happy and help others. I effectively turned myself and my young monastic students into a kind of living laboratory where we produced the sort of teaching and practices that could do that.

In the early years, the 1960s and 1970s, we produced what we called "engaged Buddhism." Together with young people, both monastic and lay, we set up an organization working to improve the quality of life of the people in the countryside. We set up the School of Youth for Social Service (SYSS) to train young monastic and lay workers to help in the areas of health, education, economics, and development. We also worked to promote peace and reconciliation. The work was difficult and dangerous, because it was being done in the midst of a horrific war. Many of our teachers and student workers were killed.

In 1974 I wrote *The Miracle of Mindfulness* as a meditation practice manual for the SYSS members. I wrote that book to help peace and social workers nourish themselves with the practice, so that they could continue serving in a situation full of suspicion and violence. That book has been warmly embraced and translated into many languages in the more than thirty-five years of its existence. In 1991 we published *Peace Is Every Step*, featuring a series of very short chapters about bringing mindfulness and peace into many different aspects of daily life. It has enjoyed even greater popularity than *The Miracle of Mindfulness*.

This book, *Peace Is Every Breath,* is a continuation of *The Miracle of Mindfulness* and *Peace Is Every Step* in that it's a short book, easy to read, and very easy to put into practice. I guarantee that you can be in touch with real peace and joy many times each day, even if you live a very full schedule. Allow this book to be your companion and live a happier life, starting now.

introduction

All of us need to have a spiritual dimension in our lives. We need spiritual practice. If that practice is regular and solid, we will be able to transform the fear, anger, and despair in us and overcome the difficulties we all encounter in daily life.

The really good news is that spiritual practice can be done at any time of the day; it isn't necessary to set aside a certain period exclusively for "Spiritual Practice" with a capital S and capital P. Our spiritual practice can be there at any moment, as we cultivate the energy of mindfulness and concentration.

No matter what you're doing, you can choose to do it with your full presence, with mindfulness and concentration; and your action becomes a spiritual practice. With mindfulness, you breathe in, and there you are, well established in the here and the now. Breathing in, touching your full aliveness, is a spiritual practice. Every one of us is capable of breathing in mindfully. I breathe in, and I know I am breathing in—that's the practice of mindful breathing.

The practice of mindful breathing may be very simple, but the effect can be great. Focusing on our in-breath, we release the past, we release the future, we release our projects. We ride on that breath with all our being. Our mind comes back to our body, and we are truly there, alive, in the present moment. We are home. Just one breath, in and out, can make us fully present and fully alive again, and then the energy of mindfulness is there in us. Mindfulness is the energy that makes us fully present, fully alive in the here and the now.

If we go home to ourselves, and if we notice that our body is carrying some tension or pain, it is mindfulness that lets us know about it. Mindfulness is what brings us back in touch with what's happening in the present moment in our body, in our feelings, in our thinking, and also in our environment. It enables us to be fully present in the here and the now, mind and body together, aware of what's going on inside us and around us. And when we are very mindful of something, we are concentrated on it.

Mindfulness and concentration are the core energies of spiritual practice. We can drink our tea in mindfulness, make our breakfast in mindfulness, and take a shower in mindfulness, and all of that becomes our spiritual practice, and gives us the strength to handle the many difficulties that can arise in our daily life and in our society.

Wherever you are, simply becoming aware of your body and whatever state of relaxation, tension, or pain (or even all of them at once, in different areas) is there, you already are realizing some understanding, some awakening, some awareness—some enlightenment. And when you know there's some tension or pain in your body, you may like to do something to help relieve it. We can say to ourselves as we breathe in and out: "Breathing in, I am aware of some tension or pain in my body; breathing out, I allow the tension and pain in my body to release." This is the practice of mindfulness of the body.

So spiritual practice is possible for all of us. You cannot say, "I'm just too busy, I have no time for meditation." No. Walking from one building to another, walking from the parking lot to your office, you can always enjoy walking mindfully, and enjoy every one of your steps. Each step you take in mindfulness can help you release the tension in your body, release the tension in your feelings, and bring about healing, joy, and transformation.

You have lots of work to do, and you like doing it. It's interesting, and you enjoy being productive. But working too much, taking care of so many things, tires you out. You want to practice meditation, so you can be more relaxed and have more peace, happiness, and joy in your life. But you don't have the time for daily meditation practice. It's a dilemma—what can you do? This book is your answer.

every
moment
is a gift
of life

waking up each morning

The moment you wake up, right away, you can smile. That's a smile of enlightenment. You are aware that a new day is beginning, that life is offering you twenty-four brand-new hours to live, and that that's the most precious of gifts. You can recite the following poem to yourself, either silently or out loud:

Waking up this morning, I smile:
Twenty-four brand-new hours are before me.
I vow to live each moment fully
and to look at all beings with eyes of compassion.

You may like to say the verse as you lie there in your bed, with your arms and legs comfortably relaxed. Breathing in, you say the first line; breathing out, you say the second. With your next in-breath, you recite the third; and breathing out, the fourth. Then with a smile on your face you sit up, slide your feet into your slippers, and walk to the bathroom.

running water, washing your face

You can be in touch with a lot of happiness during the time you're washing your face, brushing your teeth, combing your hair, shaving, and showering, if you know how to shine the light of awareness onto each thing you do. For example, when you turn on the tap, you can enjoy being in touch with the water running out of the faucet and also with where the water's coming from. You can recite the following poem:

Water flows from high mountain sources.
Water runs deep in the Earth.
Miraculously, water comes to us.
I am filled with gratitude.

This verse helps you to be aware of the whole journey of that water, all the way from the source to your bathroom sink. That is meditation. You also see how fortunate you are to have water flowing easily for you with just the twist of a knob. This awareness brings you happiness. That's mindfulness.

Mindfulness is attention; it's the capacity to recognize what's happening in each moment. What's happening here is, you are turning on the tap and the water is flowing out for you. In Plum Village, in France, our water supply occasionally gets cut off. Every time that happens, we're reminded that it's a hardship when we don't have water, and a happiness when we do. We can recognize happiness only when we remember the times of suffering!

I always like to turn the water on slowly; cup the fresh, cool water in my hands; and splash it on my eyes. Here in France, in wintertime the water is really cold. Feeling the cold water on my fingers, my eyes, and my cheeks is so refreshing. Please be present so you can really get that sensation. Let it wake you up. Delight in it. You are happy, because you know how to treasure the gift of water and how to nourish your own gratitude.

It's the same with pouring water into the basin to wash your face. Be aware of every movement; don't go off thinking about lots of other things. The most important thing for you to do in this moment is to experience joy in each of your movements. Don't hurry to finish and go do something else. That is meditation! Meditation is offering your genuine presence to yourself in every moment. It's the capacity to recognize clearly that every moment is a gift of life, a gift from the Earth and sky. In Zen, this is known as the "joy of meditation."

brushing your teeth

Here's a challenge for you. You're going to spend one to two minutes brushing your teeth. How can you do it so that you really have happiness throughout that brief couple of minutes? Don't rush. Don't try to brush your teeth as quickly as possible and be done with it. Focus all your attention on your brushing.

You have the time to brush your teeth. You have a toothbrush, toothpaste, and teeth to brush. I'm eighty-four years old, and every time I brush my teeth, I always feel happy—you know, at my age, still having all these teeth to brush is a wonderful thing! So the challenge is to brush your teeth in such a way that you have that ease and happiness during the whole one to two minutes of brushing. If you can do that, you have succeeded; you're meditating right there.

Here's a poem you can enjoy while brushing your teeth:

Brushing my teeth and rinsing my mouth,
I vow to speak purely and lovingly.

When my mouth is fragrant with right speech,
a flower blooms in the garden of my heart.

The verses are meant to help us to bring our awareness back to what's happening in the present moment. We don't get caught in reciting the lines; if we already have mindfulness and concentration, if we really know how to dwell peacefully in the present moment already, we may be just as happy not using them at all.

showering and getting dressed

While showering, shaving, combing our hair, and getting dressed, we can practice just as when we brush our teeth. We give all our attention to what we're doing. We do it in a light and leisurely manner, for our own happiness; and we know that in that moment, washing, shaving, or combing our hair is the most important thing we have to do in life. Don't let habitual thinking carry you off to events of the past or the future, or trap you in worries, sorrow, or anger.

Simply practice mindfulness like this, and in three days you will see progress; it's just like when you practice anything—playing a musical instrument, singing, or playing ping-pong. Practice living every moment of your daily life deeply and in freedom. If that's what you really want, then what you need to do is let go of pursuing the past, the future, and all your worries, and come back to the present moment.

sitting and breathing

Some people practice sitting meditation for half an hour, forty-five minutes, or longer. Here I only ask you to sit for two or three minutes. After that, if you find your sitting meditation is too enjoyable to stop, you can just continue for as long as you like.

If you have an altar in your home, you may like to sit near it. If not, sit in any suitable spot, such as in front of a window looking outside. Sit on a cushion with your legs comfortably crossed in front of you and your knees resting on the ground; this gives you a very stable position with three points of support (your seat on the cushion and your two knees). Sitting solidly, at ease, you can sit for a long time without your legs going numb. You may want to experiment with cushions of different widths and heights until you find the one that best suits your body.

If you like, you can burn a stick of incense for a sacred atmosphere. Hold the incense in your hands serenely, and concentrate your entire being on lighting the incense and placing it into the holder. Light the incense with mindfulness and concentration. Your whole self is there, fully present, as you light the incense.

Sitting down, allow your back and neck to be in a straight line, but not rigid or tense. Focus your attention on the breath as it flows into, and then out of, your belly and chest.

> *Breathing in, I feel my breath coming into my belly and chest.*
> *Breathing out, I feel my breath flowing out of my belly and chest.*
> *Breathing in, I am aware of my entire body.*
> *Breathing out, I smile to my entire body.*
> *Breathing in, I'm aware of some pains or tensions in my body.*
> *Breathing out, I release all the pains and tensions in my body.*
> *Breathing in, I feel well.*
> *Breathing out, I feel at ease.*

You can practice with this verse many times throughout the day, at work or anytime, to bring back a feeling of spaciousness, relaxation, and refreshment.

preparing breakfast

Preparing breakfast is also a meditation practice! Boiling water; making a cup of tea or coffee; fixing a bowl of oatmeal; toasting bread; cutting up fruit; setting the table—all these actions can be done with mindfulness. Doing things with mindfulness means you perform each action with clear awareness of what's happening and of what you're doing in the present moment, and you feel happy as you do it. Mindfulness is the capacity to shine the light of awareness onto what's going on here and now. Mindfulness is the heart of meditation practice.

When you prepare a cup of tea, you are fully aware that you're preparing a cup of tea. Not thinking back over the past, not thinking ahead into the future, your mind is dwelling fully in the action of making the tea: you are mindful.

Mindfulness helps us live deeply every moment of our daily life. We all have the capacity to be mindful, but those who know how to practice it develop a much more powerful energy of mindfulness and a greater capacity to dwell peacefully in the present.

You can make the time of making breakfast a meditation, very enjoyable. If another family member or housemate is already in the kitchen starting to prepare breakfast, you can go in and help. Working together in mindfulness, practicing to live in the present moment, you turn the time of breakfast making into a joy.

eating breakfast

Let breakfast be a time of relaxed and quiet happiness. Don't read the newspaper; don't turn on the television; don't listen to the radio. Sit up beautifully, and look at the food on the table. Look at each person sitting there with you, breathe, and smile as you acknowledge and appreciate them.

You can say a few words to the people at the table with you. For example: "It's great to have you sitting here at breakfast with me, Mom!" or, "The weather is beautiful today, Dad, so remember to go outside and lie in the hammock for me," or, "Sweetheart, I'm going to finish work a little earlier today, so I can be here to help you fix dinner." These kinds of comments acknowledge the precious presence of the people you love; they are a practice of mindfulness. With mindfulness, the whole exchange during breakfast time can help you and your loved ones to recognize and cherish the many conditions of happiness that you do have. After breakfast, cleaning the table and washing your bowl can be a joy before you move into the rest of your day.

thich nhat hanh

handling negative habits

We have negative mental habits that come up over and over again. One of the most significant negative habits we should be aware of is that of constantly allowing our mind to run off into the future. Perhaps we got this from our parents. Carried away by our worries, we're unable to live fully and happily in the present. Deep down, we believe we can't really be happy just yet—that we still have a few more boxes to be checked off before we can really enjoy life. We speculate, dream, strategize, and plan for these "conditions of happiness" we want to have in the future; and we continually chase after that future, even while we sleep. We may have many fears about the future because we don't know how it's going to turn out, and these worries and anxieties keep us from enjoying being here now.

Your meditation practice here is to *bring your mind back to the present* and just recognize the habit every time it pulls you away. You only need to breathe mindfully and smile to your habit energy: "Oh, I got pulled away by that again." When you can recognize habit energies

dear habit energy
i see you!

this way, they lose their hold on you, and you're free once again to live peacefully and happily in the present.

When you first start to practice, you'll catch yourself following this habit many times a day. Dwelling happily in the present is another kind of habit—a good habit. It takes a little training to acquire a new, positive habit. While brushing your teeth, washing your hair, getting dressed, walking, driving, and so on, put your full attention into what you're doing, and find the peace and joy in that very moment. When you practice conscious breathing, you have a greater ability to recognize your habit, and every time you do, its power to pull you out of the moment diminishes. It's the beginning of your liberation, your true freedom, your real happiness.

This meditation practice is known as "simple (or bare) recognition." "Dear habit energy of mine, I see you; I know you are manifesting." You don't need to do battle with it, and you don't need to suppress it; you only need to recognize it. Mindfulness is the energy that can recognize whatever is occurring, including your own negative habit energies coming up.

you are free
to be here

breaking out of the prison of the past

Some people are consumed with thoughts and memories from their past. Their mourning, regretting, rehashing, and begrudging doom them to life imprisonment in their painful past. They cannot live the present moment, as free persons. The reality is that the past is gone; all that's left of it now is impressions or images lingering in the depths of our consciousness. Yet these images from the past continue to haunt us, block us, and otherwise influence our behavior in the present, causing us to say and do things we don't really want. We lose all our freedom.

Mindful breathing lets us see clearly that the abuse, threats, and pain we had to endure in the past *are not happening* to us now, and we can abide safely here in the present. Breathing mindfully, we know the events playing out in these mental movies are not real, and simply remembering that fact removes their power to push us around.

It's like when you're flying in an airplane. Whenever severe turbulence comes along, the seatbelt keeps you from getting thrown around the cabin. Mindful breathing is your seatbelt in everyday life—it keeps you safe here in the present moment. If you know how to breathe, how to sit calmly and quietly, how to do walking meditation, then you have your seatbelt and you're always safe. You're free to be here, in touch with life, not manipulated by the ghouls of suffering from events that are over and done.

If in the past you were brutalized, abused, or otherwise made to suffer, you should know the way to practice so you can see that although those things did happen, now you are safe; you're not in any danger anymore. Recognizing the ghosts of the past for what they are, you can tell them directly that they're not real, and liberate yourself from the prison of the past. If you practice breathing, walking, sitting, and working in mindfulness for a few weeks, you will succeed at this, and those old traumas won't drag you down anymore.

walking meditation

Walking meditation is a wonderful practice that helps us be present for each moment. Every step made in awareness helps us get in touch with the wonders of life that are here, available to us right now. You can coordinate your steps with your breathing as you walk very normally along a sidewalk, a train platform, or a riverbank—wherever you are. As you breathe in, you can take a step and contemplate, "I have arrived; I am home."

"I have arrived" means *I am already where I want to be—with life itself—and I don't need to rush anywhere, I don't have to go looking for anything more.* "I am home" means *I've come back to my true home, which is life here in the present moment.* Only this present moment is real; the past and the future are only ghosts that can drag us into regrets, suffering, worries, and fear. If each of your steps brings you back to the present, those phantoms have no more power over you.

Breathing out, you may like to take three steps and continue to say to yourself, "I have arrived; I am home."

You have arrived at your true home and the wonders of life that are there for you; you don't need to wander around looking for something more. You stop running. In Zen, this is called *samatha* meditation, which means "stopping." When you can stop, your parents, your grandparents, and all your ancestors in you also can stop. When you can take a step as a free person, all your ancestors present in every cell of your body are also walking in freedom. If you can stop running and take all your steps freely like that, you are expressing the most real and concrete love, faithfulness, and devotion to your parents and all your ancestors.

I have arrived, I am home
in the here, in the now.
I am solid, I am free.
In the ultimate I dwell.

This meditation verse helps you be able to dwell solidly in the present moment. Hold fast to these words, and you'll be able to establish your presence solidly in the present, just as when you hold on to a railing while climbing stairs, you never fall.

each
step
brings you
back to
life

"In the here, in the now" is the address of *life*. It's the place we come back to—our true home—where we feel peaceful, safe, and happy, the place where we can be in touch with our ancestors, our friends, our descendants. Meditation practice is for us to keep coming back to that place. Each step brings us back to life in the present moment.

Please try practicing slow walking meditation and see for yourself. As you breathe in, take a step and say, "I have arrived." We have to invest 100 percent of our body and our mind in our breathing and our step, to be able to say we have arrived and we are home. If your mindfulness and concentration are solid, you can arrive 100 percent and be completely at home wherever you are.

If you have not yet really come back home 100 percent to the here and now, then don't take another step! Just stay right there and breathe until you can stop the wandering of your mind, until you really have arrived 100 percent in the present moment. Then you can smile a smile of victory, and take another step, with the phrase "I am home."

Solid steps such as these are like impressions of the royal seal on a king's decree. Your foot is imprinting, "I have arrived; I am home" on the Earth. Walking like this generates the energies of solidity and freedom. It puts you in touch with the wonders of life. You are nourished; you are healed. I know people who have been able to heal a number of illnesses just through practicing walking meditation wholeheartedly.

"I am solid; I am free" means you're not being pulled back by ghosts from the past and you're not being dragged into the future; you are the master of yourself. To say these words is not autosuggestion or wishful thinking. When you're able to dwell in the present, you truly do have solidity and freedom. You're free from the past and the future, not rushing around like someone possessed. Solidity and freedom are the foundation of real happiness.

Solidity and freedom
are the foundation
of true happiness

taking refuge

The Buddha taught that there's a very safe place we can come back to, no matter where we are and anytime we want. That place is the island of our true self. Within ourselves there is a safe island we can come back to, where the storms of life cannot shake us. One of the Buddha's most widely quoted phrases is *attadipa saranam,* which means taking refuge (*saranam*) in the island (*dipa*) of self (*atta*).

When you come back to your mindful breathing, you come back to yourself, and you touch the safe island inside of you. In that place you find your ancestors, your true home, and the Three Jewels. The Three Jewels are the Buddha (the teacher who shows us the way in life—it can be Jesus, Muhammad, or whoever you consider to be your guiding light), the Dharma (the teachings and the way to understanding and love), and the Sangha (our spiritual community of friends who support us on our path).

Breathing mindfully, you are already finding a refuge in your breath, and you become aware of what's going on in your body, your feelings, your perceptions, your mental formations, and your consciousness. In Buddhism, these are known as the five *skandhas* ("aggregates"), or elements, that make up what we call a person.

Mindful breathing brings all the different aspects of yourself back together as one. As you breathe, your body, your feelings, your perceptions, mental formations, and consciousness all connect with that breathing, just as if you were to lift your voice in song and everyone in your family would stop their chattering and listen! The breath calms and unifies your body and mind and harmonizes the five *skandhas* of your person. In that moment, the island of your true self is manifesting as a safe space for all five *skandhas*.

The full poem for this practice is here. In Plum Village, we have put this poem to music and we enjoy reciting it as a song:

Being an island unto myself,
Buddha is my mindfulness, shining near, shining far.
Dharma is my breathing, guarding body and mind.

I am free.
As an island unto myself,
Sangha is my five skandhas *working in harmony.*
Taking refuge in myself, coming back to myself,
I am free.
Breathing in, breathing out,
I am blooming as a flower,
I am fresh as the dew.
I am solid as a mountain,
I am firm as the Earth.
I am free.
Breathing in, breathing out,
I am water reflecting what is real, what is true;
And I feel there is space deep inside of me.
I am free.

You can practice with this verse in times of difficulty and danger, when you need to keep your cool to know what to do and what not to do. For instance, suppose you're sitting in an airplane, and suddenly you hear an announcement that the plane is being hijacked. Rather than panicking and doing things that may make the situation even more dangerous, you come back to your breathing and start to practice the first line of this poem.

The presence of mindfulness is the presence of the Buddha illuminating the situation, so you can know what to do and what not to do. Mindful breathing is the presence of the Dharma, guarding your body and your mind. Your five *skandhas* are taking refuge in the Buddha and the Dharma, receiving their protection, and representing the Sangha, serene, at peace, harmonized into one reality by your breath. With the Buddha, the Dharma, and the Sangha protecting you, you have nothing more to fear. In this calm and focused state, you will know what actions to take in order to stabilize the situation.

In more ordinary moments, practicing with this poem increases our solidity, peace, and happiness. This is the concrete practice of taking refuge in the Three Jewels, because when we practice, the energies of the Buddha, Dharma, and Sangha are genuinely there for us. There can be no greater security than that. Even facing death, we can die peacefully.

blooming as a flower, fresh as the dew

To be happy we need to have a certain amount of freshness. Our freshness can make others happy as well. We
really are flowers in the garden of humanity. We only
need to look at a child playing or sleeping, and we can
see he is a flower. His face is a flower; his hand is a flower;
his foot, his lips are flowers. We too are flowers, just like
him; but perhaps we've allowed ourselves to get weighed
down by life's hardships and lost much of our freshness.
The sixteenth-century Vietnamese sage Nguyen Binh
wrote:

No more crying, no more complaining,
This is the last brooding poem.
When you quit complaining, your soul will be
*   refreshed.*
When you stop crying, your eyes will be clear
*   again.*

Please breathe in, relax your body, and give yourself a smile! The worry lines on your face soften, and the smile on your lips brings your flowerness back again. Sculptors across the centuries have striven to portray a fresh smile of gentle compassion on the faces of their Buddha statues.

On your own face are dozens of muscles, and every time you get worried, upset, or angry, those muscles can contort or tense up; other people see that and may be scared off. Breathing in, you can bring a nonjudgmental awareness to those tensions, and breathing out, you can relax them a little bit and smile. As you continue, the tensions will dissolve in the ebb and flow of your breath, and you'll be able to restore the freshness of the human flower that is always there, available, within you. Calming, relaxing, and refreshing: these are the practices of "stopping" in Zen meditation.

Breathing in, I see myself as a flower.
Breathing out, I feel fresh.

solid as a mountain

We can't have peace and happiness without some stability. When our body and mind are unstable, we get restless and agitated, and other people don't feel they can take refuge in us or rely on us. So the practice of bringing stability and solidity to body and mind is essential.

Breathing mindfully, sitting calmly, you can reestablish solidity inside. When you sit in either the full-lotus or half-lotus position, your body and mind are stable, especially as you reunify your five *skandhas* through conscious breathing. (The five *skandhas,* once again, are the body, feelings, perceptions, mental formations, and consciousness.) If you can keep your attention focused on your breathing, you have a firm foundation for recognizing everything that's going on inside, and for accepting and embracing it. Using your intelligence and your compassion, you'll be able to find your way out of any difficulty that arises in daily life. This gives you greater confidence in your own capability, making you even more solid.

Solid
as a mountain

Breathing in, I see myself as a mountain.
Breathing out, I feel stable and solid.

Practicing to come back and take refuge in the island within helps you generate greater stability. You have a spiritual path, and you know you're walking it, so you have nothing more to fear—and this helps you be even more solid. Your path is the path of developing mindfulness, concentration, and insight—the path of the Five Mindfulness Trainings. These five trainings, or precepts, guide us toward protecting life, sharing with those in need, refraining from engaging in unwholesome sexual activities, listening deeply and using loving speech, and consuming mindfully with compassion for body and mind (see Appendix).

water reflecting

The image of a reflecting pool of water represents a tranquil mind. When the mind is not disturbed by mental formations like anger, jealousy, fear, or worries, it is calm. Visualize a clear alpine lake reflecting the clouds, the sky, and the mountains around it so perfectly that, if you were to photograph its surface, anyone would think you had taken a photo of the landscape itself. When our mind is calm, it reflects reality accurately, without distortion. Breathing, sitting, and walking with mindfulness calms disturbing mental formations such as anger, fear, and despair, allowing us to see reality more clearly.

In the *Sutra on the Full Awareness of Breathing,* one of the exercises recommended by the Buddha is called "calming mental formations." In this case "mental formations" specifically means negative states of mind such as jealousy, worry, and so on. "Breathing in, I recognize the mental formations present in me." We can call the mental formations we see by their names: "This is irritation"; "this is anxiety"; and so forth. We don't seek to suppress them, judge them, or push them away. Simply recognizing their presence is sufficient. This is the practice of bare recognition; we don't hang on to anything passing through our mind, and we don't try to get rid of it, either.

"Breathing out, I calm these mental formations." Breathing mindfully as we recognize and embrace the mental formations, we're able to give them a chance to calm down. This is similar to the exercise presented earlier in this book for calming the body, i.e., releasing the tensions and pain that are there in the body, which also was taught by the Buddha in the *Sutra on the Full Awareness of Breathing*.

You are a meditation practitioner, which means you actually practice looking deeply and contemplating, and not just learning about Zen as an intellectual or theoretical object of study. So you should train yourself to calm disturbing mental formations and emotions when they manifest. Only in this way will you be able to master your body and mind and avoid creating conflicts within yourself and with your loved ones and others.

riding out the storm

Some young people are unable to cope with the storms of emotion that rise up in them, like rage, depression, despair, and so forth, and they want to kill themselves. They're convinced that suicide is the only way to stop their suffering. In the United States, approximately 9500 young people commit suicide every year, and the rate is even higher in Japan. It seems no one is teaching them the way to handle their strong emotions.

If we can show them the way to calm down and free themselves from the grip of suicidal thinking, they'll have a chance to come back and embrace life again; but we need to get the practice down for ourselves before we try to show others. We don't wait until we're overwhelmed by some emotion to start practicing. Start now, so that the next time a wave of emotion comes up, you'll know how to take care of it.

First of all, you need to know that an emotion is only that—an emotion—even though it may be a big, strong one. You are so much bigger, so much more than this emotion. Our person—the territory of our five *skand-has* (body, feelings, perceptions, mental formations, and consciousness)—is immense. Emotions are but one category of the many different mental formations we can have. They come, they stay for a while, and then they go. Why should we have to die for an emotion?

Look at strong emotions as a kind of storm. If we know weatherproofing techniques, we can come out of it intact. A storm may last an hour, several hours, or a day. If we master the ways of calming and steadying our mind, we can pass through the storms of emotion with relative ease.

Sitting in the lotus position or lying down on your back, begin breathing into your belly. Keep your mind entirely on the belly as it rises with every in-breath and falls with each out-breath. Breathe deeply, maintaining full attention on your abdomen. *Don't think.* Stop all your ruminating, and just focus on the breathing. When trees get hit by a storm, the treetops are thrashed around and run the highest risk of being damaged. The trunk of a tree is more stable and solid; it has many roots reaching deep into the Earth. The treetops are like your own head, your thinking mind.

When a storm comes up in you, get out of the treetop and go down to the trunk for safety. Your roots start down at your abdomen, slightly below the navel, at the energy point known as the *tan tien* in Chinese medicine. Put all your attention on that part of your belly, and breathe deeply. Don't think about anything, and you'll be safe while the storm of emotions is blowing. Practice this every day for just five minutes, and after three weeks, you'll be able to handle your emotions successfully whenever they rise up.

Seeing yourself pass through a storm unharmed, you gain more confidence. You can tell yourself, "Next time, if the storm of emotions comes back, I won't be scared or shaken, because now I know the way to overcome it." You can teach this to kids as well, so they too can enjoy the sense of safety that belly breathing can give them. Take the hand of your child, and tell her to breathe with you, putting all her attention on her abdomen. Though she may be only a child, she can have very strong emotions, and she can learn to breathe her way through them. At first, she will need your assistance, but later on she'll be able to do it herself. If you're a schoolteacher, you can teach abdominal breathing to all the students in your class. If at least some of your students use the practice, then later, when the whirlwind of strong emotion starts churning inside them, they won't be driven to commit suicide; and you will have saved lives.

Practicing in the sitting position is best, but you can also practice while lying down. If you're practicing while lying down, you may like to place a hot-water bottle on your abdomen as an added source of comfort.

having space

Space represents freedom and ease. Without freedom, how can we be happy? So: What has made you lose your freedom? Getting caught up in worries, overwork, jealousy . . . ?

Maybe you believe that being successful in attaining power, wealth, and recognition is what will make you happy. But if you pause to examine that notion, you'll see there are people who have plenty of money, fame, and influence, but still aren't happy. Why? Because they don't have real freedom.

You have many things to do, and you want to succeed in every area. There's nothing wrong with that. But you should arrange your life so that your work truly brings you happiness each day. Don't lose yourself in work and let it get you worried, irritated, or down. Work in freedom. You should still have enough time for yourself and for the people close to you. You should have time to love. By "love" here I'm not talking about the excitation of sensual desire; I'm talking about having the time to care for others, to do things that make them happy and help relieve their suffering.

The most precious gift you can offer to the people you love is a sense of spaciousness—space around, and space inside. Don't get carried away from real life by busyness, troubles, and disappointments. Know how to shake off the worries and live joyfully. This is an art. Practice to let go of unimportant things that don't bring any happiness. When you can let go, you have more space.

Imagine a fellow who goes to a flea market, sees a bargain, and brings it home even though he doesn't need it. He sees a low price, and he just buys. In a few weeks his house is so filled with all this stuff, he can hardly get in or out. Anytime he tries to move around the place, he bumps into another item he brought home from the market. He has no more space to live. The same is true of our mind. If we have too many worries, fears, and doubts, we have no room for living and loving. We need to practice letting go.

Breathing in, I see myself as space.
Breathing out, I feel free.

Buddhism teaches that joy and happiness arise from letting go. Please sit down and take an inventory of your life. There are things you've been hanging on to that really are not useful and deprive you of your freedom. Find the courage to let them go. An overloaded boat is easily capsized by wind and waves. Lighten your load, and your boat will travel more quickly and safely. You can offer the precious gift of freedom and space to your loved ones, but only if it is truly there in your own heart.

understanding and loving

The practice method known as contemplating with loving-kindness and compassion can bring great ease and happiness. Loving-kindness is bringing happiness to other persons; compassion means relieving their suffering. The key that opens the door to loving-kindness and compassion is our capacity to understand our own suffering and difficulties, and the suffering and difficulties of others. If we can see and understand our own suffering, then we easily can see and understand the difficulties of the other person, and vice versa.

This is the practice of looking deeply into the first and second of the Four Noble Truths, the four sacred and wonderful truths of Buddhism. The Four Noble Truths are: first, there is suffering; second, there is a path or a series of conditions that has produced the suffering; third, suffering can be ended—happiness is always possible; and fourth, there is a path that leads to the cessation of suffering, to happiness. Recognizing and acknowledging our difficulties (the first Noble Truth), then looking deeply into them and their root causes (the second truth), we are able to see the way out, the path of liberation (the fourth truth); the transformation and cessation of suffering accomplished by taking that path is the third Noble Truth.

Here's an example of how the practice works. A father is making his son suffer. The father doesn't see that he's causing suffering to his son, and to himself as well. He really believes that the way he's treating his son is for the best. In reality, it is not so.

The reality is that the father has a lot of difficulties and hurts, but he has yet to see them (the first Noble Truth: the acknowledgment of suffering) and look into their root causes (the second Noble Truth: the path that leads to suffering). He doesn't know how to deal with his own suffering, he makes his son suffer, and he believes his son is the one causing all the unhappiness.

Perhaps from a very young age the father was subjected to cruel mistreatment by his own father, the grandfather. The grandfather poured out all his anger and suffering on this father; and now the father is doing as the grandfather did, pouring out his anger and pain on his son. The wheel of *samsara* turns again and again, as the suffering gets passed down from one generation to the next. The father doesn't see the second Noble Truth, the source of his suffering. Now is the time for the son to practice:

Breathing in, I see myself as a five-year-old child.
Breathing out, I smile to the five-year-old child still
*   alive and present in me.*
Breathing in, I see the five-year-old child in me is
*   fragile, vulnerable, wounded.*
Breathing out, I embrace the five-year-old child in me
*   with all my understanding and love.*

This is the first part of the practice, coming back to yourself to recognize and embrace the little child inside of you. For so long now, you've been too busy to do this. Now you come back to talk with, listen to, and embrace that child. The healing process can begin.

my father in me,
my mother in me

When you have practiced the first part successfully, you can move on to the second part:

Breathing in, I see my father as a five-year-old child.
Breathing out, I smile to my father, five years old.

Perhaps you never have imagined your own father as a tender little boy. The truth is that your father was once fragile and vulnerable, easily hurt, just like every other little child.

Breathing in, I see my father, five years old, fragile,
*   vulnerable, wounded.*
Breathing out, I look at this wounded child with all
*   my understanding and love.*

Many people have had painful difficulties in the relationships with their parents. You may not have realized until now that the five-year-old child who became your father is still here today, present in you, as well as in him. Both your father and your mother have transmitted nothing less than their entire selves to you. As a matter of fact, you and your father are not two entirely different people, even though you're not exactly one and the same person either. The same is true of you and your mother. This wonderful insight may be called "Not one, not two"—neither exactly the same nor entirely different.

If you can embrace the five-year-old child inside one of you, you can embrace the child inside the other as well, and then the transformation of your relationship can happen very quickly. If only your father had had the chance to learn this when he was young, he would not have caused himself and you to suffer. But he was not so fortunate; so you have to practice, for yourself and also for your father in you. When you can transform your father inside of you, you will be able to help your father outside of you to transform much more easily. Practicing in this way we can effect a transformation in ourselves as well as in our parents, and avoid repeating the same mistakes with our own children. The wheel of suffering is brought to a stop at last.

This deep understanding of suffering and its root causes gives rise to acceptance and love. When we can love and accept, we feel much better, and we also will be able to help other people transform—an uncle or aunt, a brother or sister, a colleague or a friend.

In you there is the seed of a mental formation called *prajna,* "insight." It means profound understanding. When profound understanding is there, the situation changes immediately. *Prajna* is, first of all, seeing and understanding whatever suffering is there, and the nature, the source, of that suffering. Practicing looking deeply using the above exercises, we increase our capacity for deep insight. We should invite that capacity to be present with all the activities of our mind; but sometimes we forget or we don't really apply ourselves in using it, especially when the passions are inflamed. At that moment, we need the intervention of mindfulness. Mindfulness is the mental formation that is most essential and needed for our practice. We should remember that mindfulness always brings insight. When we have insight, we very naturally are more accepting, forgiving, loving, and happy. When we lack insight, we veer off in the direction of anger, jealousy, hatred, and suffering.

awareness of the store consciousness

Everything we see, hear, think, and experience gets stored away in the depths of our consciousness. The Buddha called this our *store consciousness*. Our store consciousness—comparable to what Western psychologists call the subconscious—receives, processes, and retains all kinds of data. Our joys, worries, fears, and frustrations are all retained in this great archive. It's like the hard disk of our mental computer. Mental formations like concerns and expectations may not be apparent or manifesting at a particular moment, but they are ever present in the depths of consciousness in the form of dormant seeds. In Buddhist psychology the mental formations are known as *anusaya*.

These seeds, though sleeping, are always ready to reactivate, sprout up, and take over your mind. They pull data out from the archive and replay past experiences on the screen of your consciousness, dragging you back through old events and depriving you of real life in the present moment. Things you really do see or hear in the present may be the initial trigger, but once those old stories have been accessed, have risen up and taken center stage in your mind, you lose touch with the things you actually are seeing and hearing. Eventually you end up living most or all of your life inside the virtual world of your own memory instead of in the real world. The world inside your head is far removed from the world as it really is; yet you are quite convinced that your illusory world is the real one.

Those films from the store consciousness are often replayed in your dreams at night. The dormant seeds are many and varied, and the contents of the films likewise may vary, even though all come from the same archive. In dreams you experience apprehension, anxiety, love, hatred, expectation, achievement, disappointment, and so on. You move about in that dream world just like in normal life, and you believe it's all real. Then, waking up, you discover you actually have been lying in your bed asleep the whole time. Those dream worlds and the person moving through them are the products of your own consciousness, assembled from the archives of your mind.

During the daytime, although you're wide awake, you still can slip frequently into the illusory world of the subconscious—sometimes for just a few seconds, sometimes for a whole hour. In fact, you rarely *truly* live in the real world, and your views of the real world are strongly influenced by your store consciousness. Practicing to walk and breathe mindfully helps you dwell more in the real world, so you can get in touch with the wonders of life in the present moment, and nourish and heal your body and mind.

Each step is a miracle.
Each step is healing.
Each step is nourishing.
Each step is freedom.

inappropriate attention

There is right mindfulness, and there is wrong mindfulness. We know already that right mindfulness is the energy that can bring us back to the present moment in order to recognize what's going on. On the other side is wrong mindfulness, the energy that pulls us into dwelling on the painful past, into focusing and clinging to pain, worry, suffering, craving, fear—the toxic items in the store consciousness. When you can see clearly that you've gotten caught in a negative story from the past, right mindfulness has already begun to operate. It tells you what's going on: you're getting carried away by a story from the past. Your awareness instantly frees you from the mirage and brings you back to the real world.

In dreams, the things you see, the objects of your consciousness, are only images; they have no substance. It's like when you snap a photo of your dog with a digital camera. From the moment you press the button on the camera, the image of your dog is recorded on the memory card, frozen in time, while your real dog continues to jump, play, and bark. The picture you took isn't the dog; it's just a recorded image. In reality your dog could have grown old and died already, but your image remains forever fixed and unchanging, in your store consciousness just as in your camera.

When you're in touch with real life, what you directly see, hear, and touch is taken in by your sense organs, forming sense impressions. These impressions are still relatively close to reality, though they also may be colored somewhat by the contents of your store consciousness. But if you close your eyes and call the images back up in your mind, at that point they will be experienced only as what we call "mere images."

Your subconscious is filled with images, and you may find yourself returning to some of them as a kind of security blanket or comfort zone, even if they're painful memories. It's the same kind of morbid desire that makes people want to listen over and over again to tragic songs of mourning over loss and grief. It's a habit that isn't healthy or productive.

that old, familiar, mucky pond

Some people are unable to leave their painful past behind, to live freely and at ease among the wonders of life in the present. The moon and stars are glowing brightly, the mountains and streams are delightful, the four seasons reveal themselves to us by turns; but some never get in touch with any of that. They feel more comfortable hanging around the cellar of their painful memories.

Liberation means, first of all, breaking out of the prison of our past. We need to summon the courage to pull ourselves back up out of the rut of our old, familiar habits and comforts. These things don't really bring us happiness; but we've gotten so used to them, we think we can't let them go. Why must we, as the Vietnamese expression goes, always come back to swim in the same old pond, even though it's mucky, simply because it's "ours"? Why deprive ourselves of the crystal clear lake, of the refreshing blue sea with a beach stretching all the way to a new horizon? The joys of life are no less "ours." We need to train ourselves in right mindfulness, so that wrong mindfulness doesn't keep on dragging us back into the past, keeping us stuck in the slimy old pond of sorrow, nostalgia, and regret.

We know the mind can have that "homing pigeon" tendency of always going back to old, familiar haunts of pain and misery. Mindfulness—recognition—helps us drop that habit of continually reliving the past. Tell yourself, "No: I don't want to go back into that again. I don't want to keep lulling myself into melancholy with those old songs." As soon as we light up the lamp of right mindfulness, wrong mindfulness retreats.

Meditation includes cultivating awareness of mental formations like yearning, sadness, self-pity, resentment, and so on. If we recognize and embrace these mental formations when they come up, they no longer can carry us away. They go back down again, a little bit weaker than before, to their original state as seeds or images in the store consciousness.

appropriate attention

We have six sense organs that can be in contact with the world outside, and with all the "worlds" inside. The six organs are our eyes, ears, nose, tongue, body, and mind. These organs are like sensors hooked up to a computer. When you get in touch with an image, a sound, a smell, a taste, a touch, or a thought, your mind receives that signal and immediately goes through material stored in the subconscious, searching for any connection to the sensory input. Almost instantaneously the archived material you access becomes the actual object of your mind, producing mental formations such as worry, suffering, fear, craving, or anger.

"Attention" is directing our mind to an object of one of our six senses. We should direct our attention only to sense objects that connect us with archives producing positive mental formations such as freedom and ease, joy, brotherhood/sisterhood, happiness, forgiveness, and love. This is what's called "appropriate attention." When, on the other hand, we focus on sense objects that call up images and experiences of pain, sorrow, fear, and craving, that is inappropriate attention.

The environment in which we live and work plays a very important role in this practice. When we choose wholesome living and working environments (and that includes the things we hear, see, smell, and touch), they help us get in touch with what's beautiful and healthy in us and in the world, and we will be nourished, healed, and transformed. We should do everything we can to choose—or create—wholesome environments for ourselves, our children, and our grandchildren. If you are a political leader, if you work in a ministry of culture, or if you are a teacher or a parent, please reflect on this point.

food is the gift
of the whole
universe

mindful consumption

Mindful consumption means choosing to consume things that bring peace and happiness, rather than agitation and harm, to our body and mind (see the fifth of the Five Mindfulness Trainings in the Appendix). When we look deeply, we know how to nourish our body and mind with wholesome foods and avoid taking in harmful ones. In Buddhism, we speak of four kinds of food that our body and mind may take in: edible food, sense impressions, volition, and consciousness.

Edible food is food that enters through our mouth. We really are what we eat! In Asia the people say, "Illness enters through the mouth." The French say, "We dig our graves with our teeth." It's well known that a large percentage of deaths, whether from heart attack, diabetes, or other diseases, are directly related to the way we eat. When we eat and drink mindfully, we don't put unhealthy things in our body just because they're tasty, because we know the momentary pleasure will lead to bigger suffering later on. We can recite one or more of these five contemplations before eating:

This food is the gift of the whole universe: the Earth, the sky, numerous living beings, and much hard work.

May we eat with mindfulness and gratitude, so as to be worthy to receive this food.

May we recognize and transform unwholesome mental formations, especially our greed, and learn to eat with moderation.

May we keep our compassion alive by eating in such a way that we reduce the suffering of living beings, preserve our planet, and reverse the process of global warming.

We accept this food so that we may nurture our sisterhood and brotherhood, build our community, and nourish our ideal of serving all living beings.

At least once a week, we should remind ourselves of our desire to eat mindfully by reciting these five contemplations at our family meal.

Sense impressions are the kind of food that we take in with our eyes, ears, nose, tongue, body, and mind. Certain kinds of music, newspaper articles, films, websites, electronic games, and even conversations can contain a lot of toxins like craving, violence, hatred, insecurity, fear, and so on. Consuming these kinds of poisons harms our mind and also our body.

Volition is our deep motivation, our deepest desires; it's the energy that moves us day and night to do the things we do. Meditation includes looking deeply into the nature of these deepest desires. If a desire is coming from a beautiful ideal, like ending poverty, hatred, and division among individuals, groups, and nations or promoting liberty, democracy, human rights, and social justice, that is a wholesome volition that can bring happiness to us and to the world. The desire to practice to transform afflictions in us such as violence, hatred, and despair, and generate more love, understanding, and reconciliation, is a good desire to have. When we are able to realize such aspirations in our own life, we can help other people in society to do the same. This is a wholesome kind of volition.

If, instead, we're being driven by an urge to punish and take revenge on those who've hurt us or to destroy those we believe to be our enemies, that is a harmful volition. If our motivation is just to get lots and lots of money, power, fame, and sex, this type of volition will also bring suffering. Our happiness depends largely on what kind of volition we're picking up on and acting out. Running after objects of craving can do a lot of damage to our body and mind.

Consciousness, the fourth category of food, here refers to the collective consciousness in which we live and which we thereby consume through a kind of osmosis. Our concepts of happiness and of beauty and our views on matters of ethics, morality, and manners are largely the product of the collective consciousness that surrounds us. We may have cultivated good taste and beautiful ideals in ourselves and our family, but we could lose them if we go to live in a place where everyone has tastes and habits that are different from ours. At first we feel uncomfortable, but after a while we become accustomed to the ideas of the majority, and in the end we're following the crowd without even realizing it.

The widowed mother of the future philosopher Mencius woke up to this reality one day when she saw her son pretending to do violent acts with his friends in the street, and she made the effort to move to a more wholesome environment for her son. Living among people who have wholesome minds, we can nourish and protect the best qualities in our own minds, and with a strong collective consciousness like that we can help to change and transform our society.

The *Sutra on the Four Kinds of Food* (sometimes called the *Sutra on the Son's Flesh*) is an excellent sutra and very much needed in our society today. It shows us the way out of the sickness and suffering of our society, which is consuming far too many toxic things, like violence, hatred, and despair.*

---

*You may like to go more deeply into this very important subject by reading my recently published book, *Savor: Mindful Eating, Mindful Life*.

mindfulness
is not
for sale

shopping for happiness

Mindfulness is the most precious asset we can have; it makes love, happiness, and so many other gifts to ourselves and to others possible. But it's not for sale in any shop, no matter how much money we're prepared to pay for it. We have to produce it ourselves.

We can't just go to the store to buy some mindfulness and bring it home with us; but we can and do want to take our mindfulness with us when we go shopping. We already know we want to consume only things that bring joy and health to ourselves and our society, and we need the energy of mindfulness to keep us on track as we pass by one enticing display after another. Mindfulness helps us to recognize—more and more clearly the longer we practice—which things we really need and want in our life, and which things we can do very well without. We're able to spend far less money on "stuff" without sacrificing any of our happiness. In fact, we have more happiness, because we can take a less stressful, more enjoyable job when we're not under the financial pressure of constantly having to buy newer, bigger, and fancier houses, cars, and other things.

So: you need to buy some things, and you don't have lots of time to do it. How can you stay present and not be seduced by clever advertising? How can you choose products that don't compromise your own health and don't promote exploitation of human workers, of animals, of our planet?

Whether you're shopping in a store or online, try not to do it when you're hungry, tired, or distracted. Make a list in advance of the things you need. The short time it takes to do this will be more than compensated for by the time you'll save by not having to debate whether to buy additional things you don't need and maybe don't even really want. Before you check out, take a moment to look back over the things in your basket and ask yourself honestly: "Do I really need this? Will buying this bring me more happiness than giving that money to help relieve the suffering of another living being?"

dwelling happily in the present

Breathing and walking with awareness generates the energy of mindfulness. This energy brings our mind back to our body so that we're really here in the present moment, so we can be in touch with the wonders of life that are there inside us and around us. If we can recognize these wonders, we have happiness immediately. Fully available to the present moment, we discover that we already have enough conditions to be happy—more than enough, in fact. We don't need to go looking for anything more in the future or in some other place. That's what we call abiding or dwelling happily in the present.

The Buddha taught that every one of us can live happily right here and now. When we have happiness in the present moment, we can stop; we don't need to run after any more objects of desire. Our mind is calm. When our mind is not yet calm, when it's still agitated, we can't really be happy. Our happiness or lack of happiness depends mostly on the state of our mind, not on anything external. It's our own attitude, the way we look at things, our approach to life, that determines whether we're happy or not. We have plenty of conditions to be happy already, so why should we have to go searching for more? We need to stop and not go chasing after another lure—that's the wiser course. Otherwise, we keep pursuing this goal or that one, but every time we attain it, we find we still aren't happy.

One day when the Buddha was going to speak at the Jeta Grove monastery, the Buddha's lay disciple Anathapindika, a businessman, brought a few hundred colleagues with him to hear the Buddha speak. The Buddha taught them the practice of dwelling happily in the present. Of course we can go on doing business, and we can continue to realize increasing success in our career; but we also should commit ourselves to living mindfully, so we can enjoy being happy right *now,* and not miss out on the precious opportunities life is handing us to love and care for our near and dear ones. If we spend all our time just thinking about our future successes, we completely miss out on life, because life can only be found in the present moment.

the kingdom of god is now—or never

We should be able to enjoy the wonders of life in us and everywhere around us. The whispers of rustling pine boughs. Flowers blooming. The beautiful blue sky. Fluffy white clouds. The smile of a neighbor. Each of these is a small miracle of life that has the capacity to nourish and heal us. They're there for us right now. The question is: are we there for them? If we're constantly running around, if our mind is caught up in endless planning and worrying, it's as if all these wonders don't even exist.

The Kingdom of God, the Pure Land of the Buddha is right here. We should practice to enjoy the Kingdom with every step we take. We ought to enjoy our happiness right now, today; tomorrow may be too late. There's an old French song that asks, *Qu'est-ce qu'on attend pour être heureux? Qu'est-ce qu'on attend pour faire la fête?* ("What are we waiting for to be happy? Why wait to celebrate?") Meditation is the practice of living deeply each moment of daily life. To do it, we need to be able to generate mindfulness and concentration with our breathing and our steps.

Mindfulness is being aware of what's happening in the present moment; concentration is maintaining that attention. With mindfulness and concentration, we can look deeply into and understand what's happening. We can pierce the veil of ignorance, see clearly the true nature of reality, and be liberated from the anxiety, fear, anger, and despair in us. That is insight. Mindfulness, concentration, and insight are the very essence of meditation.

concentrating the mind

In the *Sutra on the Full Awareness of Breathing,* the Buddha offered a series of sixteen deepening exercises to practice with our breathing. The eleventh exercise is "concentrating the mind." When our mindfulness is well established, we can go deeply into concentration. Concentration is the focusing of the mind. It is the energy that helps us look really deeply into whatever we're contemplating, whether it's a flower, a cloud, a pebble, a loved one, an enemy, or a feeling such as hope or despair. Concentration empowers us to see into the true nature and the origins of the object of our contemplation. When we can really focus our mind, it becomes like a magnifying glass in the sunlight, capable of burning away many wrong views that are fueling anger, anxiety, craving, and despair.

To help us succeed in liberating ourselves through this practice of looking deeply, the Buddha offered as tools the contemplations on impermanence, no-self and emptiness, signlessness and no-birth/no-death, aimlessness, and wishlessness, among others. We can choose one or two contemplations to begin practicing with—for example, impermanence and no-self.

contemplating impermanence

You may have already understood the concept of impermanence and accepted it as reality, but is that taking place only on the intellectual level? In your everyday life, do you still act as if things are permanent? Understanding the *notion* of impermanence is not enough to change the way you experience and live your life. Only the *insight* can truly emancipate you, and that insight cannot arise unless you really practice looking deeply into impermanence. That means maintaining your awareness of impermanence all the time and never losing sight of it, in everything you do. It means *concentrating* on impermanence, and keeping that concentration alive throughout the day. As the awareness of impermanence pervades your being, it illuminates your every act in an extraordinary new way and brings you real freedom and happiness.

For example, you know the person you love is impermanent, but you go on acting as if that person is permanent, expecting he or she will be there forever in the same form, with the same outlook and the same perceptions. Meanwhile, the reality is just the opposite: that person is changing, in appearance as well as inside. Someone who's there today might not be there tomorrow; someone who's strong and healthy today might fall ill tomorrow; someone who's not very nice today may become a much nicer person tomorrow; and so on.

Only when we've taken this reality fully into our being, can we live our lives really skillfully and appropriately. Seeing that the people we know are impermanent, we'll do whatever we can today to make them happy, because we never can know if they'll still be there tomorrow. They're still there right now, but if we are not kind to them, perhaps one day they will leave.

If you're angry at someone for having made you suffer, and you're about to say or do something hurtful in retaliation, please close your eyes, breathe in a long, deep breath, and contemplate impermanence:

Feeling the heat of anger right now,
I close my eyes and look into the future.
Three hundred years from now,
where will you, where will I, be?

This is a visualization practice. You see what both you and the person you want to punish will be three hundred years from now: dust. Touching deeply the impermanence of yourself and the other person, seeing clearly that in three hundred years both of you will be dust, you know right away that getting angry with each other and making each other suffer is a foolish, tragic waste. You see that the presence of that person in your life right now is a treasure. Your anger dissolves; and when you open your eyes, you no longer want to punish. All you want to do is hug that person close.

Contemplating impermanence helps you break free from the chains of anger. By concentrating your mind, you can liberate it.

this is in that
and that is in this

contemplating no-self and emptiness

In the section entitled "My Father in Me, My Mother in Me" above, we contemplated the presence of the parent in the child, seeing how the child is the continuation of the parent, how the child *is* the parent, and how the happiness of the child is also the happiness of the parent, and the suffering of the parent is also the suffering of the child. When we can maintain awareness of this, we are contemplating no-self. There is no entity separate and apart from everything else; what we call our "self" is made entirely of "non-self" elements.

Emptiness likewise refers to the absence of a self that exists apart from everything else—the way a flower, for example, cannot "be" by itself alone, but rather is made of non-flower elements such as the seed, fertilizer, rain, and sunlight. If you take the non-flower elements out of the flower, the flower no longer can exist. Emptiness does not mean nothingness or nonexistence; it only means there is no such thing as a separate "self" entity.

All phenomena rely on all other phenomena to manifest. This is, because that is; this is not, because that is not. To contemplate emptiness is also to contemplate interbeing (sometimes called "interdependent co-arising"). This is in that, and that is in this. This is that. This does not exist without that.

contemplating signlessness, no-birth and no-death

The purpose of contemplating signlessness is to help us avoid getting caught in the trap of external appearances. Where there is a sign, there is deception; the Buddha spoke about this in the *Diamond Sutra*. Water vapor, for instance, is there in front of us right now; just because we can't see it, that doesn't mean it doesn't exist. When a cloud turns into rain, we cannot rightly say the cloud has gone from being to nonbeing. We don't see water vapor, but as soon as it meets up with some cold air, it will turn into fog or frost that we can see; and we can't say that that fog or frost has come into a state of "being" from one of "nonbeing." It has simply changed its form, the sign by which we label it.

No-birth is another way to describe the true nature of reality, the nature of all that is. When we look at the outer appearances of things, we see birth and death, success and failure, being and nonbeing, coming and going. But when we look more deeply, we see the true nature

---

just because we
can't see it
that doesn't mean
it doesn't exist!

---

of things is unborn and undying, not coming from any-where or going anywhere, neither being nor nonbeing, not all one single entity yet not really separate and apart.

The cloud did not become something from nothing. Before it manifested in its current form, it was already there as water in the rivers and oceans. With the sun's heat it became water vapor, and then those tiny droplets came together as a cloud. It didn't pass from "nonbeing" into "being." This is the meaning of no-birth.

Later, the cloud may cease that manifestation and assume other forms, such as rain, snow, hail, fog, or a little creek. The cloud will not have gone from "being" to "nonbeing." Its nature is not only unborn, but also un-dying. The real nature of the cloud and of all that is, including you and me, is unborn and undying.

Once the insight of no-birth and no-death has arisen in you, you will experience fearlessness and a tremen-dous freedom. That is truly the most precious fruit of meditation.

We are
already
what we want
to become

contemplating aimlessness

Contemplating aimlessness helps us stop feeling compelled to go around seeking after this and that, exhausting ourselves mentally and physically. Aimlessness means not chasing after anything, not setting any more objects in front of ourselves to run after. Happiness is available right in this present moment. We already are what we want to become.

It's like a wave who goes looking to get in touch with the vastness of water. When she realizes water already is her own true nature, her very substance, she no longer needs to go looking elsewhere for it. Everywhere you turn, life is full of wonders. The Kingdom of God, the Pure Land of the Buddha, is already right here, within and all around us; and the same is true of happiness. Contemplating aimlessness helps us be able to stop our rushing around and experience a sense of contentment and joy.

contemplating wishlessness

Contemplating wishlessness means looking deeply into the objects of our desires. When we do this, we can see the dangers, disasters, and distress that chasing after desires can bring. When a fish sees a fat, juicy worm wriggling in front of his face, if he knows there's a sharp hook buried inside that worm, he will not bite into it, and his life will be saved. When we remember that we're much more, much greater, than our cravings, we can tap into the part of ourselves that knows we already have all we really need. Contemplating wishlessness preserves our freedom, so that we never have to become victims of the objects of craving. Thanks to that freedom, we can live at ease, in peace and happiness.

true love
brings only
happiness
it never makes you suffer

boundless love

True love brings only happiness; it never makes you suffer. In Buddhism, we see that it's understanding that gives rise to true love. When we don't understand the person to whom we're offering what we think is love, the more we love, the more we make that person suffer. As we have seen already, understanding is first of all being able to see the sources of pain and suffering in oneself and in the other person. A father who hasn't understood the difficulties and suffering of his children cannot really love them and make them happy. He will keep scolding and trying to control them, making them suffer. When we think we're loving someone but we don't really understand him, we end up hurting him.

We should ask ourselves: Have I been able to understand the difficulties and the suffering of that person yet? Have I been able to see the sources of that suffering? If the answer is not yet "yes," then we need to make more of an effort to understand. "My son, my daughter, do you think I've understood your difficulties, your stresses, and suffering well enough? If not, please help me understand you better. I know that if I haven't really understood you, then I can't really love you and make you happy. Please, help me. Tell me about the difficulties and the pain inside of you." This is the practice of loving speech.

In Buddhism, we learn that if we can understand our own suffering, we easily will be able to understand the suffering of others. So we should come back to ourselves first and get in touch with the suffering inside of us, and not give in to the urge to run away from it or numb ourselves into forgetting about it. In the Buddha's most fundamental teaching on the Four Noble Truths, the first truth is about recognizing the suffering that is there, and the second truth is looking into the nature and the root sources of that suffering.

Once we've been able to see into the roots of the suffering, we can see the way to transform it, that is, the path leading to transformation and ending of the suffering. That is the fourth truth. The third truth refers to the result, the actual cessation of the suffering—or, in other words, the presence of happiness. The absence of suffering is happiness, just as the absence of darkness is the presence of light. The teaching on the Four Noble Truths is a core teaching in Buddhism and a wonderful,

highly practical one. It's the Buddhist method for diag-
nosing and healing what ails us.

Buddhism also teaches that we have to love ourselves
before we truly can love anyone else. Only when we've
been able to relieve our own suffering will we be able to
help relieve someone else's. We need to have some happiness before we can offer it to others to help them be
happy too. The French have a saying: *Charité bien or-
donnée commence par soi-même* ("The right charity begins with oneself"). Offering happiness is the practice of
loving-kindness, the first of the four elements of true love
in Buddhism.

The second of the four elements, *compassion,* is about
relieving suffering. Loving-kindness and compassion
are boundless. Through our practice, loving-kindness
and compassion are nourished, and they can embrace
our whole self, then another person, and ultimately all
beings. Loving-kindness and compassion are sometimes
called "immeasurable minds" and are two elements of
the love that knows no bounds. The other two of the
four immeasurable minds, or four elements of true love,
are *joy* and *nondiscrimination* (*equanimity*).

True love brings joy, a sense of delight and fulfillment.
If your love feels stifling, if it makes you or your loved

We have to love
ourselves
before we can truly
love anyone else

one cry all the time, that is not true love. Our presence, our words, our actions, and even our thoughts should bring joy and delight. The other person's joy is our own joy; her delight and satisfaction are our own delight and satisfaction. We are happy for her happiness; her success is our own success; her freedom and ease are our own freedom and ease.

Practicing mindfulness, we can recognize all the conditions of happiness that are there, the many happy moments we are living, and this brings us quite naturally into a state of joy. Mindfulness brings us happiness. Concentration makes that happiness even greater, stronger, and more solid.

Equanimity means not drawing lines, not taking sides, not discriminating, not rejecting. True love has to be like that—not discriminating based on skin color, race, or religion; not excluding anyone. This is the highest love, the love that can embrace every human and every living thing. It is the love of the Buddha. When we love in this way, we see no boundary between the lover and the one who is loved; we and our beloved are not separate entities. With equanimity, our love becomes truly boundless love.

deep, compassionate listening

Deep listening is a meditation practice that can bring many miracles of healing. Think of a person with difficulties and suffering in his heart which no one has been able to listen to or understand. We can be the bodhisattva, the person animated by great compassion for all beings, who sits and listens deeply in order to relieve the suffering of that person. We should use our mindfulness to remind ourselves that when we offer someone our practice of deep listening, we do it with the sole aim of helping them empty their heart and release their pain. When we can stay focused on that aim, we can continue to listen deeply, even when the other person's speech may contain a lot of wrong perceptions, bitterness, sarcasm, judgment, and accusation.

Listening deeply with all of our heart, with all our loving-kindness and compassion, we don't get irritated by anything the other person says. We say to ourselves: "Poor him, he has a lot of wrong perceptions, he's burning up with rage and hurt." We keep listening; and then

patience
is one
of the
marks
of true
love

later on, when a good opportunity presents itself, we can provide the other person with more accurate information to help him see the reality more clearly. Anger and suffering are born from wrong perceptions; when we can get a more accurate picture of reality, the black cloud of anger and suffering dissolves. Knowing this, we can sit calmly and continue listening attentively.

We allow the other person to say everything that's on her mind; we encourage her to pour everything out, and we don't interrupt her or try to correct her in that moment. One hour of deep listening like this can reduce the other person's suffering a great deal and help her feel much lighter. Patience is one of the marks of true love. We should wait and find the right moment later on to begin offering some information that will help the other person correct her wrong perceptions. And we don't try to give the information all at once, because she may not be able to digest all that in one big chunk, and might reject it entirely. We should offer the information in measured doses, small enough that she can take them in and eventually be released from the grip of all those wrong perceptions. Listening nonjudgmentally also gives us an opportunity to discover and correct our own wrong perceptions, and when this happens, we can apologize to the other person straightaway.

In Buddhism, the *bodhisattva* Avalokiteshvara (also known as Quan Yin in Chinese, Kannon in Japanese, or Quan The Am in Vietnamese) is the specialist in listening with loving-kindness and compassion. Here is a recitation for this practice, from the daily chanting book we use in Plum Village:

> We invoke your name, Avalokiteshvara. We aspire to learn your way of listening in order to help relieve the suffering in the world. You know how to listen in order to understand. We will sit and listen without any prejudice. We will sit and listen without judging or reacting. We will sit and listen in order to understand. We will sit and listen so attentively that we will be able to hear what's being said and also what's being left unsaid. We know that just by listening deeply, we already alleviate much pain and suffering in the other person.

loving speech

Loving speech is also a meditation practice. We have the right and the responsibility to tell the whole truth, all our thoughts and feelings, including our difficulties and our suffering. But we don't use words of judgment, blame, bitterness, or irritation; we use the language of love. We speak only of our own difficulties and suffering, so the other person can understand and help us. We acknowledge that we probably have some wrong perceptions, and we ask the other person to help us to see them and provide us with the more accurate information that we lack. This practice of loving speech, together with the practice of compassionate listening, has the capacity to reestablish communication and build deep, nourishing relationships. Writing a letter with mindful, loving words can bring a great deal of transformation and healing, not only to the receiver, but to the sender as well.

taking care of anger

When the energy of irritation or anger arises, as practitioners we should immediately come back to conscious breathing and do some walking meditation, to produce the energy of mindfulness so we can recognize and take care of that anger.

> *Breathing in, I know anger is manifesting in me.*
> *Breathing out, I'm taking good care of this energy of anger in me.*

We continue practicing in this way to generate the energy of mindfulness, to recognize and embrace the energy of anger.

We should never let the energy of anger go on swelling up all by itself, unattended; we need to call up our energy of mindfulness to come and take care of it. Mindfulness is like a mother who comes to embrace her suffering, crying baby. Our anger is just like a crying baby. When the mother picks up the distraught baby and tenderly holds him in her arms, the child starts to feel better already. When anger is embraced by mindfulness, it too begins to calm down.

Any time your anger rises up, please practice in this way, and don't try to say or do anything about the situation yet. Imagine you've been away from your house, doing some errands, and now you've just come back and found your house on fire. The first thing you need to do is not to take off running through the neighborhood to find the arsonist, berate him, and bring him to justice. The first thing you need to do is deal with the burning fire in your house, so it doesn't go on to destroy everything. When anger is flashing up in you, don't give in to the urge to start speaking and acting it out. Come back to your breathing and take care of your emotions first.

As the anger starts to calm down, we can begin looking into its root causes. Perhaps a wrong perception has triggered it. Maybe we're convinced that someone deliberately did or said something to upset us, when in fact they didn't mean to. After some reflection we may recognize our wrong perceptions, dissipating the anger. If, after twenty-four hours of practicing like this, we still have not found our way out, we need to let the other person know what's going on. If we're not able to do this calmly in person, we can write a note. We should say three things:

1. I'm angry with you, and I want you to know it.

2. I am doing my best to practice.

3. Please help me.

Already after writing down these three sentences, even before the note is received, our anger will go down a little bit.

When we're upset, we have a responsibility to let the other person know. The other person may be our father or mother, our sister or brother, our son or daughter, our friend, colleague, or co-worker. When the other person knows we're upset, she will look back and think, "What have I done? What have I said to upset him?" So our three sentences also act as a skillful invitation for the other person to take this opportunity to practice, too. And that person will appreciate and respect you for not acting out your anger, as many other people might do, and for knowing how to practice when you're angry, taking the time to come back to your mindful breathing and reflect on the situation.

The third sentence is the most difficult one to say or write, because when we're angry, we have the tendency to want to punish the other person by showing that we don't need her at all. Instead of doing that, we should find the courage to ask for the other person's help. We know the truth—we do need her—and we mustn't let pride block our way forward through difficult situations. So whenever you manage to say or write that third sentence, you already can see your suffering start to go down.

Please write these three sentences down on a piece of paper the size of a credit card and put it in your wallet. When you get angry, and especially if you're angry with the person you love the most, take it out and read it. Then even if you're still in the grip of anger, you'll know exactly what you want to do—and not do. Thousands of people are now doing this practice and, through it, have been able to reconcile many difficulties. I wish you every success!

your every breath

As you breathe in, you take a few steps; and during those seconds you notice that you are alive, that your legs and feet are still strong enough to walk (and climb, and run). You realize that to be alive, and walking on this beautiful planet, is already a miracle. And you can delight in that miracle as you walk. That's the miracle of mindfulness and concentration. In any moment, you can touch the miracle of life, and become joyful and happy right where you are.

When we can recognize the many conditions of happiness that are there, in us and around us, we realize that we don't need to be searching for happiness anywhere else, or hoping it will arrive on some future day. This is very important, to know that happiness is possible here and now. With mindfulness you can recognize all the conditions of happiness that are already in you and around you, more than enough for you to be happy. I think the same insight may be found in the Bible and other sacred scriptures.

If you know how to be happy with the wonders of life that are already there for you to enjoy, you don't need to stress your mind and your body by striving harder and harder, and you don't need to stress this planet by purchasing more and more stuff. The Earth belongs to our children. We have already borrowed too much from it, from them; and the way things have been going, we're not sure we'll be able to give it back to them in decent shape. And who are our children, actually? They are us, because they are our own continuation. So we've been shortchanging our own selves.

Much of our modern way of life is permeated by mindless overborrowing. The more we borrow, the more we lose. That's why it's critical that we wake up and see we don't need to do that anymore. What's already available in the here and now is plenty for us to be nourished, to be happy.

Only that kind of insight will get us, each one of us, to stop engaging in the compulsive, self-sabotaging behaviors of our species. We need a collective awakening. One Buddha is not enough. All of us have to become Buddhas in order for our planet to have a chance.

Fortunately, we have the power to wake up, to touch enlightenment from moment to moment, in our very own ordinary and, yes, busy lives. So let's start right now. Peace is *your* every breath.

gathas
for daily
practice

*G*athas are short verses that we can recite during our daily activities to help us return to the present moment and dwell in mindfulness. As exercises in both meditation and poetry, *gathas* are an essential part of Zen Buddhist tradition. Using a *gatha* doesn't require any special knowledge or religious practice. Some people like to memorize a favorite verse that they find they can come back to again and again. Others just like to write the verse down in a place they are likely to see it often.

The use of *gathas* goes back over two thousand years. When I entered the Tu Hieu Monastery in Vietnam as a novice in 1942, I received a copy of *Gathas for Everyday Use,* compiled by the Chinese meditation master Du Ti. Du Ti's book of fifty *gathas* was written for monks and nuns of former times. At Plum Village, where I live in France, we practice *gathas* when we wake up, when we enter the meditation hall, during meals, and when we wash the dishes. In fact, we recite *gathas* silently throughout the entire day to help us attend to the present moment. One summer, in order to help the children and adults at Plum Village practice mindfulness, we began assembling *gathas* relevant for life today. The result is this collection of practical, down-to-earth verses.

We often become so busy that we forget what we are doing or even who we are. I know people who say they even forget to breathe! We forget to look at the people we love and to appreciate them, until it is too late. Even when we have some leisure time, we don't know how to get in touch with what is going on inside and outside of ourselves. So we turn on the television or pick up the telephone, as if we might be able to escape from ourselves.

To meditate is to be aware of what is going on—in our bodies, our feelings, and our minds and in the world. When we settle into the present moment, we can see beauties and wonders right before our eyes—a newborn baby, the sun rising in the sky. We can be very happy just by being aware of what is in front of us.

Reciting *gathas* is one way to help us dwell in the present moment. When we focus our mind on a *gatha*, we return to ourselves and become more aware of each action. When the *gatha* ends, we continue our activity with heightened awareness. When we drive a car, signs can help us find our way. The sign and the road become one, and we see the sign all along the way until the next sign. When we practice with *gathas,* the *gathas* and the rest of our life become one, and we live our entire lives in awareness. This helps us very much, and it helps others as well. We find that we have more peace, calm, and joy, which we can share with others.

When you memorize a *gatha,* it will come to you quite naturally when you are doing the related activity, whether it's turning on the water or drinking a cup of tea. You don't need to learn all the verses at once. You can find one or two that resonate with you and learn more over time. After some time, you may find that you have learned all of them and are even creating your own. When I wrote the *gathas* for using the telephone, driving a car, and turning on the computer, I did so within the tradition that I inherited from my teachers. You are now one of the inheritors of this tradition. Composing your own *gathas* to fit the specific circumstances of your life is one wonderful way to practice mindfulness.

I hope you find this collection of *gathas* a steady and delightful companion.

Waking Up

Waking up this morning, I smile.
Twenty-four brand-new hours are before me.
I vow to live fully each moment
and to look at all beings with eyes of compassion.

Taking the First Step of the Day

Walking on the Earth
is a miracle!
Each mindful step
reveals the ultimate dimension.

Opening the Window

Opening the window, I encounter the ultimate.
How wondrous is life!
Attentive to each moment,
my mind is clear like a calm river.

Turning on the Light

Forgetfulness is the darkness,
mindfulness is the light.
I bring awareness
to shine upon all life.

Turning on the Water

Water flows from high mountain sources.
Water runs deep in the Earth.
Miraculously, water comes to us.
I am filled with gratitude.

Brushing Your Teeth

Brushing my teeth and rinsing my mouth,
I vow to speak purely and lovingly.
When my mouth is fragrant with right speech,
a flower blooms in the garden of my heart.

Looking in the Mirror

Awareness is a mirror reflecting the four elements.
Beauty is a heart that generates love
and a mind that is open.

Using the Toilet

Defiled or immaculate,
increasing or decreasing—
these concepts exist only in our minds.
The reality of interbeing is unsurpassed.

Washing Your Hands

Water flows over these hands.
May I use them skillfully
to preserve our precious planet.

Bathing

Unborn and indestructible,
beyond time and space—
both transmission and inheritance of this body
reflect the oneness of all that is.

Washing Your Body

Rinsing my body,
my heart is cleansed.
The universe is perfumed with flowers.
Actions of body, speech, and mind are calmed.

Getting Dressed

Putting on these clothes,
I am grateful to those who made them
and to the materials from which they were made.
I wish everyone could have enough to wear.

Greeting Someone

A lotus for you,
a Buddha to be.

Following the Breath

Breathing in, I calm my body.
Breathing out, I smile.
Dwelling in the present moment,
I know this is a wonderful moment.

Morning Meditation

The Dharma body radiates this morning.
In concentration, my heart is at peace. A half-
    smile is born upon my lips.
This is a new day.
I vow to go through it in mindfulness.
The sun of wisdom has now risen, shining in
    every direction.

Entering the Meditation Room

Entering the meditation room,
I see my true self.
As I sit down,
I vow to cut off all disturbances.

Lighting a Candle

Lighting this candle,
offering the light to countless Buddhas,
the peace and joy I feel
brighten the face of the Earth.

Offering Incense

In gratitude, we offer this incense to all
Buddhas and bodhisattvas
throughout space and time.
May it be fragrant as Earth herself,
reflecting our careful efforts,
our wholehearted awareness,
and the fruit of understanding, slowly ripening.
May we and all beings be companions
of Buddhas and bodhisattvas.
May we awaken from forgetfulness
and realize our true home.

Praising Buddha

As refreshing as a lotus flower,
as bright as the North Star:
to the Buddha
I go for refuge.

Sitting Down

Sitting here is like sitting under
the Bodhi tree.*
My body is mindfulness itself,
calm and at ease,
free from all distraction.

Inviting the Bell

Body, speech, and mind in perfect oneness—
I send my heart along with the sound of the bell.
May the hearers awaken from forgetfulness
and transcend all anxiety and sorrow.

*The tree under which the Buddha became enlightened.

Listening to the Bell

May the sound of this bell
penetrate deeply into the cosmos.
In even the darkest places,
may living beings hear it clearly,
so that understanding may light up their hearts
and, without hardship, they may transcend
the realms of birth and death.

Letting Go

Hearing the bell,
I am able to let go of all afflictions.
My heart is calm,
my sorrows ended.
I am no longer bound to anything.
I learn to listen to my suffering
and the suffering of the other person.
When understanding is born in me,
compassion is also born.

thich nhat hanh

Adjusting Your Posture

Feelings come and go
like clouds in a windy sky.
Conscious breathing
is my anchor.

Hugging Meditation

Breathing in,
I am so happy to hug my loved one.
Breathing out,
I know my loved one is real and alive in my arms.

Cleaning the Meditation Room

As I clean
this fresh, calm room,
boundless joy
and energy arise!

Walking Meditation

The mind can go in a thousand directions,
but on this beautiful path, I walk in peace.
With each step, a gentle wind blows.
With each step, a flower blooms.

Washing Vegetables

In these fresh vegetables
I see a green sun.
All dharmas* join together
to make life possible.

Looking at Your Empty Bowl

My bowl, empty now,
will soon be filled with precious food.
Beings all over the Earth are struggling to live.
How fortunate we are to have enough to eat.

---

*The word *dharmas* with a small "d" means all phenomena, everything
we experience as existing in the phenomenal world.

Serving Food

In this food
I see clearly
the presence of the entire universe
supporting my existence.

Looking at Your Plate

This plate of food,
so fragrant and appetizing,
also contains much suffering.

Five Contemplations for Eating

This food is the gift of the whole universe:
the Earth, the sky,
numerous living beings,
and much hard and loving work.
May we eat with mindfulness and gratitude
so as to be worthy to receive this food.
May we recognize and transform
unwholesome mental formations,
especially our greed.
May we keep our compassion alive by eating in
    such a way that we reduce the suffering of
    living beings, preserve our planet, and reverse
    the process of global warming.
We accept this food so that we may nurture
our sisterhood and brotherhood,
build our Sangha, and nourish our ideal
of serving all living beings.

thich nhat hanh

Beginning to Eat

With the first mouthful,
I practice the love that brings joy.
With the second mouthful,
I practice the love that relieves suffering.
With the third mouthful,
I practice the joy of being alive.
With the fourth mouthful,
I practice equal love for all beings.

Finishing Your Meal

My bowl is empty.
My hunger is satisfied.
I vow to live
for the benefit of all beings.

Washing the Dishes

Washing the dishes
is like bathing a baby Buddha.
The profane is the sacred.
Everyday mind is Buddha mind.

Drinking Tea

This cup of tea in my two hands,
mindfulness held perfectly.
My mind and body dwell
in the very here and now.

Touching the Earth

Earth brings us to life
and nourishes us.
Earth takes us back again.
We are born and we die with every breath.

Looking at Your Hand

Whose hand is this
that has never died?
Who is it who was born in the past?
Who is it who will die in the future?

Hearing the Bell

Listen, listen,
this wonderful sound
brings me back
to my true home.

Using the Telephone

Words can travel thousands of miles.
May my words create mutual understanding and
    love.
May they be as beautiful as gems,
as lovely as flowers.

Turning on the Television

The mind is a television
with thousands of channels.
I choose a world that is tranquil and calm,
so that my joy will always be fresh.

Turning on the Computer

Turning on the computer,
my mind gets in touch with the store.
I vow to transform habit energies
to help love and understanding grow.

Cleaning the Bathroom

How wonderful it is to scrub and clean.
Day by day,
the heart and mind grow clearer.

Sweeping

As I carefully sweep
the ground of enlightenment,
a tree of understanding
springs up from the Earth.

Watering the Garden

Water and sun
green these plants.
When the rain of compassion falls,
even the desert becomes a vast fertile plain.

Planting

I entrust myself to Earth;
Earth entrusts herself to me.
I entrust myself to Buddha;
Buddha entrusts himself to me.

Picking a Flower

May I pick you, little flower,
gift of Earth and sky?
Thank you, dear bodhisattva,
for making life beautiful.

Arranging Flowers

Arranging this flower
in a world that has difficulties we learn to bear,
the ground of my mind
is pure and calm.

Smiling at Anger

Breathing in, I feel my anger.
Breathing out, I smile.
I stay with my breathing,
so I won't lose myself.

Washing Your Feet

The peace and joy
of one toe
is peace and joy
for my whole body.

Driving the Car

Before starting the car,
I know where I am going.
The car and I are one.
If the car goes fast, I go fast.

Recycling

In the garbage, I see a rose.
In the rose, I see the garbage.
Everything is in transformation.
Even permanence is impermanent.

Ending the Day

The day is ending,
our life is one day shorter.
Let us look carefully at what we have done.
Let us practice diligently,
putting our whole heart into the path of
    meditation.
Let us live deeply each moment in freedom,
so time does not slip away meaninglessly.

the path of the buddha

The path of the Buddha is the path of understanding and love. As we've seen, only when we understand can we really love. Understanding is insight. Love is the energy of the heart. Buddhist wisdom includes the key insights of interbeing and interdependent co-arising, which have the capacity to transform all narrow-mindedness, discrimination, and hatred. The Five Mindfulness Trainings (also known as the Five Precepts) of Buddhism embody and guide us on the path of ever deepening wisdom.

If you live according to the Five Mindfulness Trainings, you will create a lot of happiness for yourself and for many others. The recently revised Five Mindfulness Trainings reprinted here are the Buddhist vision for a truly global ethic in this twenty-first century. Practicing the Five Mindfulness Trainings generates peace and joy, and gives future generations and our planet some hope of making it to the twenty-second century.

Once we have a path, we have nothing more to fear. Please look deeply into these trainings and put them into practice in your own personal life, your family life, and your society.

1. reverence for life

Aware of the suffering caused by the destruction of life, I am committed to cultivating the insight of interbeing and compassion and learning ways to protect the lives of people, animals, plants, and minerals. I am determined not to kill, not to let others kill, and not to support any act of killing in the world, in my thinking, or in my way of life. Seeing that harmful actions arise from anger, fear, greed, and intolerance, which in turn come from dualistic and discriminative thinking, I will cultivate openness, nondiscrimination, and nonattachment to views in order to transform violence, fanaticism, and dogmatism in myself and in the world.

2. true happiness

Aware of the suffering caused by exploitation, social injustice, stealing, and oppression, I am committed to practicing generosity in my thinking, speaking, and acting. I am determined not to steal and not to possess anything that should belong to others; and I will share my time, energy, and material resources with those who are in need. I will practice looking deeply to see that the happiness and suffering of others are not separate from my own happiness and suffering; that true happiness is not possible without understanding and compassion; and that running after wealth, fame, power, and sensual pleasures can bring much suffering and despair. I am aware that happiness depends on my mental attitude and not on external conditions, and that I can live happily in the present moment simply by remembering that I already have more than enough conditions to be happy. I am committed to practicing right livelihood, so that I can help reduce the suffering of living beings on Earth and reverse the process of global warming.

3. true love

Aware of the suffering caused by sexual misconduct, I am committed to cultivating responsibility and learning ways to protect the safety and integrity of individuals, couples, families, and society. Knowing that sexual desire is not love, and that sexual activity motivated by craving always harms myself as well as others, I am determined not to engage in sexual relations without true love and a deep, long-term commitment made known to my family and friends. I will do everything in my power to protect children from sexual abuse and to prevent couples and families from being broken by sexual misconduct. Seeing that body and mind are one, I am committed to learning appropriate ways to take care of my sexual energy and cultivating loving-kindness, compassion, joy, and inclusiveness—which are the four basic elements of true love—for my greater happiness and the greater happiness of others. Practicing true love, we know that we will continue beautifully into the future.

4. loving speech and deep listening

Aware of the suffering caused by unmindful speech and the inability to listen to others, I am committed to cultivating loving speech and compassionate listening in order to relieve suffering and to promote reconciliation and peace in myself and among other people, ethnic and religious groups, and nations. Knowing that words can create happiness or suffering, I am committed to speaking truthfully using words that inspire confidence, joy, and hope. When anger is manifesting in me, I am determined not to speak. I will practice mindful breathing and walking in order to recognize and to look deeply into my anger. I know that the roots of anger can be found in my wrong perceptions and lack of understanding of the suffering in myself and in the other person. I will speak and listen in a way that can help myself and the other person to transform suffering and see the way out of difficult situations. I am determined not to spread news that I do not know to be certain and not to utter words that can cause division or discord. I will practice right diligence to nourish my capacity for understanding, love, joy, and inclusiveness, and gradually transform anger, violence, and fear that lie deep in my consciousness.

5. nourishment and healing

Aware of the suffering caused by unmindful consumption, I am committed to cultivating good health, both physical and mental, for myself, my family, and my society by practicing mindful eating, drinking, and consuming. I will practice looking deeply into how I consume the four kinds of nutriments, namely, edible foods, sense impressions, volition, and consciousness. I am determined not to gamble, or to use alcohol, drugs, or any other products which contain toxins, such as certain websites, electronic games, TV programs, films, magazines, books, and conversations. I will practice coming back to the present moment to be in touch with the refreshing, healing, and nourishing elements in me and around me, not letting regrets and sorrow drag me back into the past nor letting anxieties, fear, or craving pull me out of the present moment. I am determined not to try to cover up loneliness, anxiety, or other suffering by losing myself in consumption. I will contemplate interbeing and consume in a way that preserves peace, joy, and well-being in my body and consciousness, and in the collective body and consciousness of my family, my society, and the Earth.